the book on fassforward

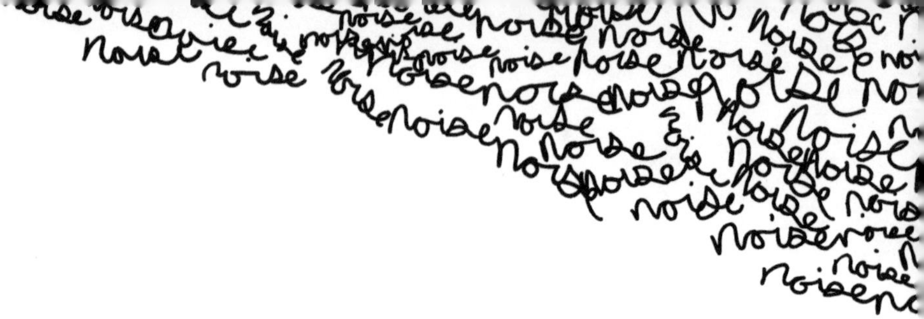

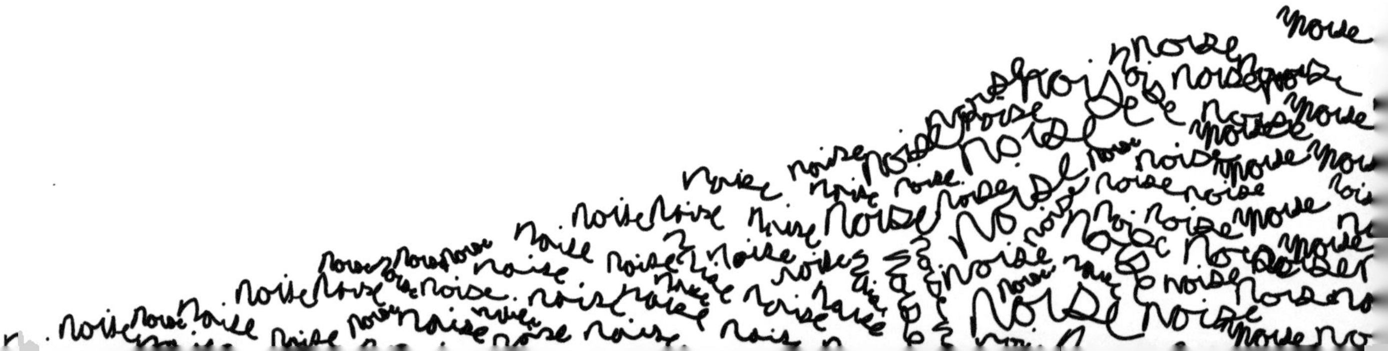

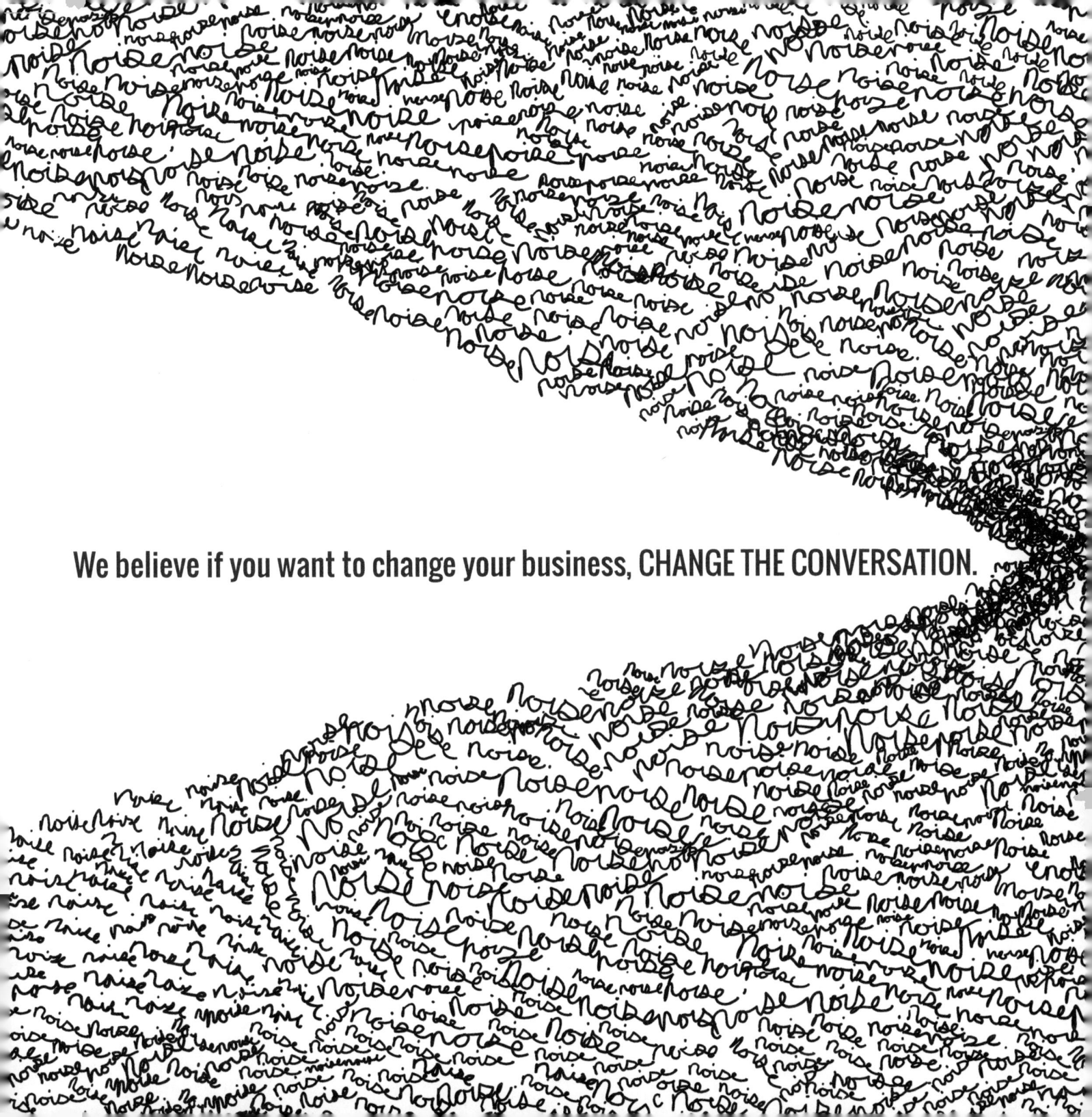

We believe if you want to change your business, CHANGE THE CONVERSATION.

Are people in your business having

Businesses have to remain relevant. Without relevance there is no growth. New strategies, acquisitions, process, and reorgs will only get you part of the way. What we've learned is that if you don't change the conversation, real change won't happen.

Relevant businesses have relevant conversations. Everything else just adds to the noise. That noise is the rhythmic lull of business as usual. It's multiple conversations taking place around the same subject — a lot of activity, little action — and conflicting views that diminish performance and dampen commitment. These are signs of what we call a Chocolate Conversation.

What is a Chocolate Conversation?

"When people are talking past each other and have completely different points of view, while believing they're on the same page."

-Rose Fass: Author,
The Chocolate Conversation

Here's the problem. Chocolate Conversations only add to the noise.

Leaders that change the conversation change the way people think and inspire them to move forward.

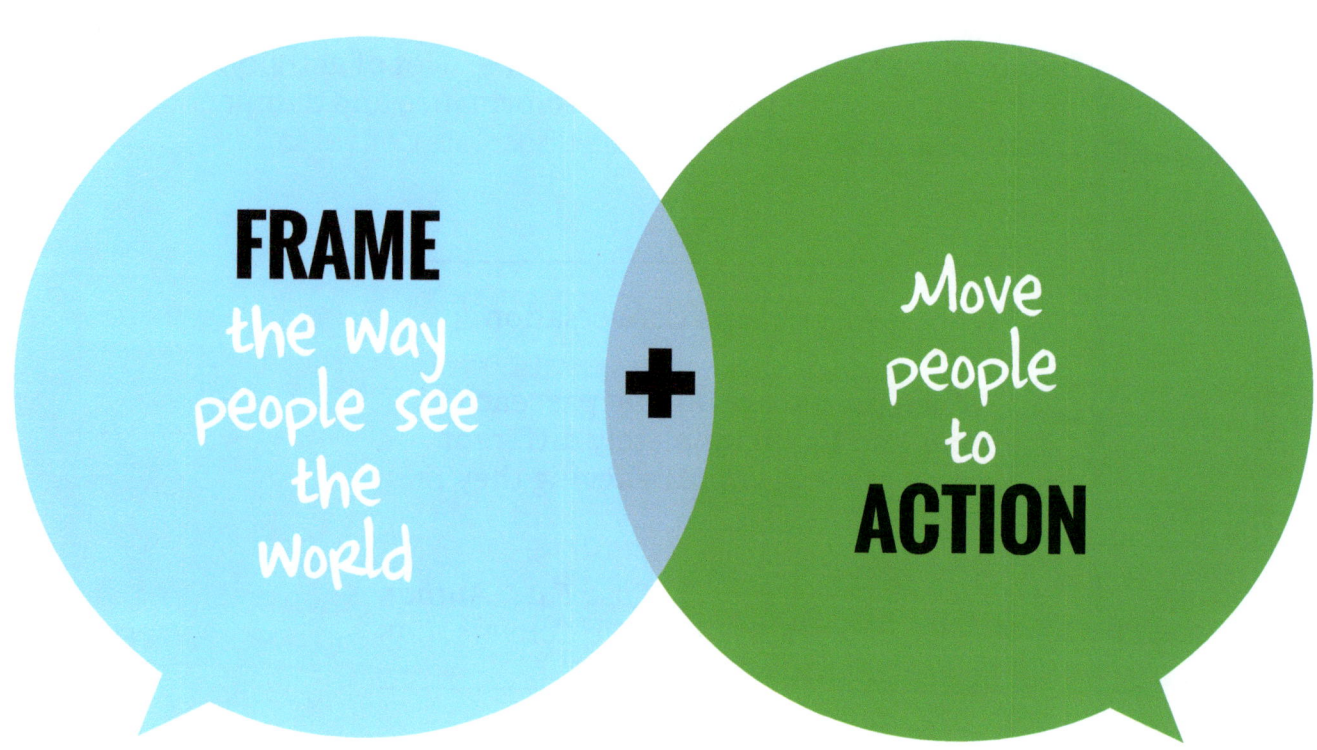

CHANGE HAPPENS IN

There are only two conversations that matter —
the conversations that frame the way people see
the world, and the conversations that move them
to action. Everything else is just noise.

THE CONVERSATION

What do
CHOCOLATE
CONVERSATIONS
cost you?

We're so used to Chocolate Conversations that we don't stop to measure the cost. We might run operations reviews on a quarterly basis to drive performance. What if they could cost 10% less and be 10% more effective? When we prepare a new strategy, do we understand how culture will complement it, or kill it?

Over $638 billion was spent on innovation last year.[1]

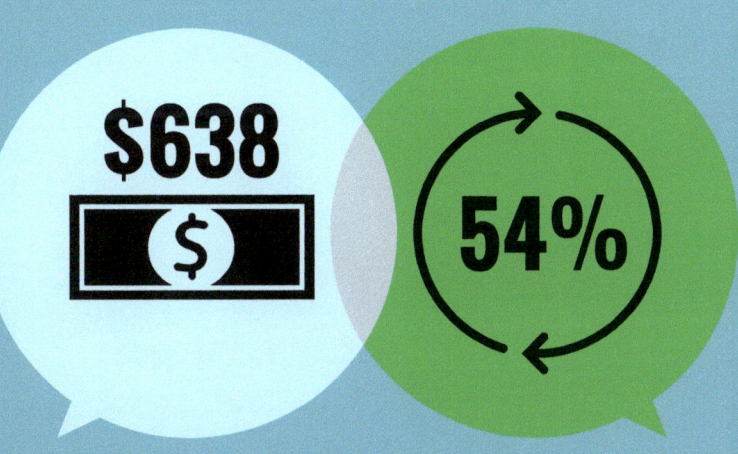

Changing the conversation can improve innovation effectiveness by up to 54%.[2]

1 The Global Innovation 1000: Navigating the Digital Future. PWC. http://www.strategyand.pwc.com/media/file/Strategyand_2013-Global-Innovation-1000-Study-Navigating-the-Digital-Future.pdf

2 Innovation in Globally Distributed Teams Gajendran & Joshi, 2012.

Fully engaged customers represent a 23% premium in wallet share, profitability and revenue.[3]

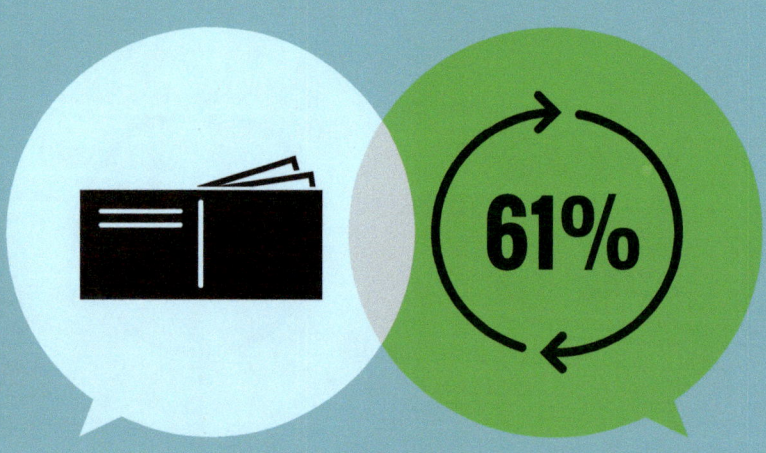

61%

Changing the conversation can improve long term customer relationships by up to 61%.[4]

3 Gallup, why Customer Engagement Matters. http://www.gallup.com/businessjournal/172637/why-customer-engagement-matters.aspx

4 Effective communication styles for the customer-oriented service employee Kang & Hyun, 2017

The average lifespan of a business on the S&P 500 has dropped from a high of 61 years to 18 years.[5]

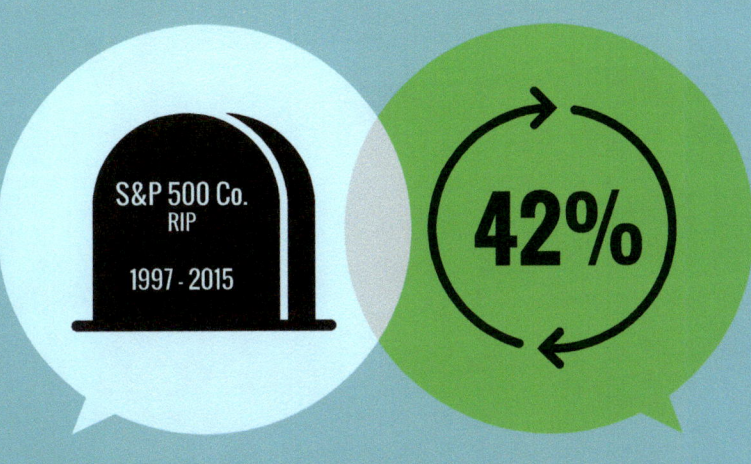

Changing the conversation can improve organizational performance by up to 42%.[6]

5 Innosight, Creative Destruction Whips Through Corporate America, 2012 http://www.innosight.com/innovation-resources/strategy-innovation/upload/creative-destruction-whips-through-corporate-america_final2012.pdf

6 Organizational Communication and Performance, 1984

Diagnose your

CHOCOLATE CONVERSATIONS

Where do they happen?

What are the symptoms?

What is the cure?

Where do they happen?

Chocolate Conversations happen in the seams: between strategy and execution, marketing and sales, service and customers.

People are talking past each other, each side nodding, thinking they're on the same page.

What are the symptoms?

Talk is cheap, but ——conversations are costly. While they manifest themselves in many ways, you will see the symptoms. It constrains future innovation and growth, confuses employees, limits company's ability to execute, damages company culture, and erodes relationships with customers and other external stakeholders.

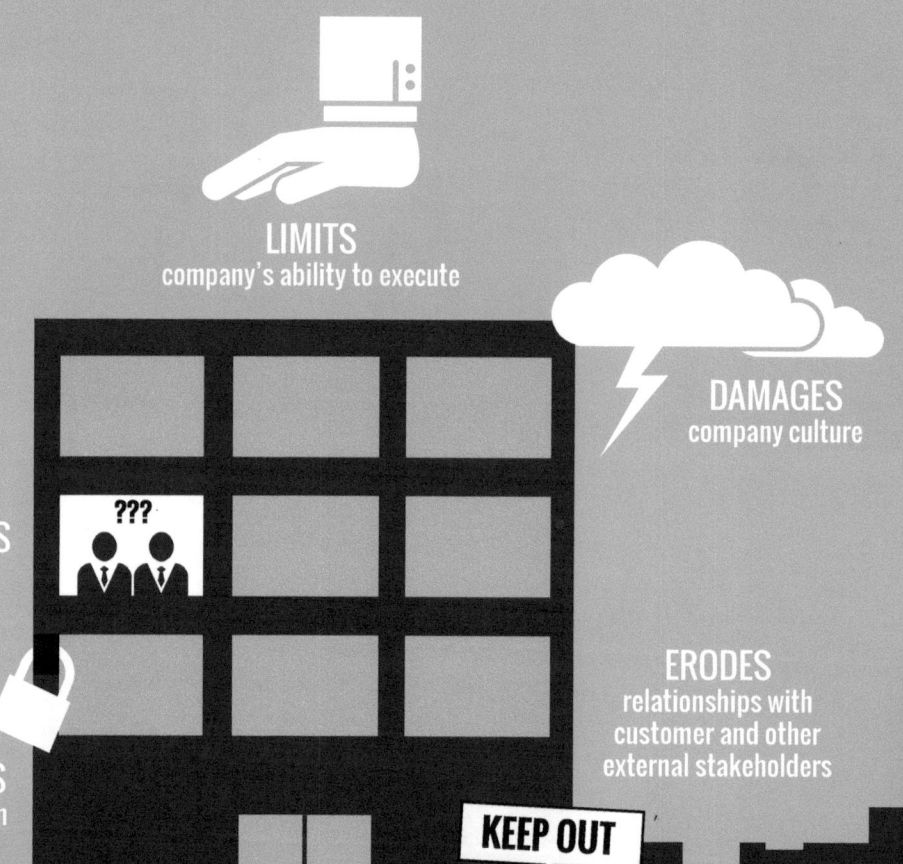

LIMITS
company's ability to execute

DAMAGES
company culture

CONFUSES
employees

ERODES
relationships with customer and other external stakeholders

CONSTRAINS
future innovation and growth

KEEP OUT

What is the cure?

The Chocolate Conversation Diagnostic examines the seams where you think Chocolate Conversations may be happening, and assesses their impact on people, process and culture. It shows where you have gaps.

CULTURE
PEOPLE
PROCESS

Noise ▶	Knowing What Matters	Truth Telling	Going There
Frame ▶	Connecting Dots	Setting Context	Translating the Message
Action ▶	Moving People	Making Things Happen	Extending Your Reach

fassforward is a consulting firm that helps leaders

CHANGE THE CONVERSATION

inside and outside the business about Culture, Innovation and Customers.

CONNECT

Conversations
for deep
understanding.

Connect with
your people to
build trust and
confidence,
and open
the door for
collaboration.

DIG-IN

Rapid insight
into the
business.

Dig-In to where
Chocolate
Conversations
are happening
and diagnose
their impact.

BUILD

Design
outcome based
experiences.

Build tailored
experiences
that get
everyone on
the same page
using simple
tools to solve
complex
problems.

ENERGIZE

Encourage
debate and
co-creation.

Energize
leaders and
teams working
side-by-side
to develop
strategies and
plans with
measurable
outcomes.

DELIVER

Make things happen.

Deliver the end goal by connecting strategy to culture and execution.

Our method is simple and scalable.

"We operate in the seams and gaps where conventional forces can't go."

- Major Eric Wright,
US Special Forces Commander

We're not claiming to be special forces. But we are like them in one respect — we operate in the seams where conventional thinking, and conventional consultants and agencies don't go.

Cut through the noise.

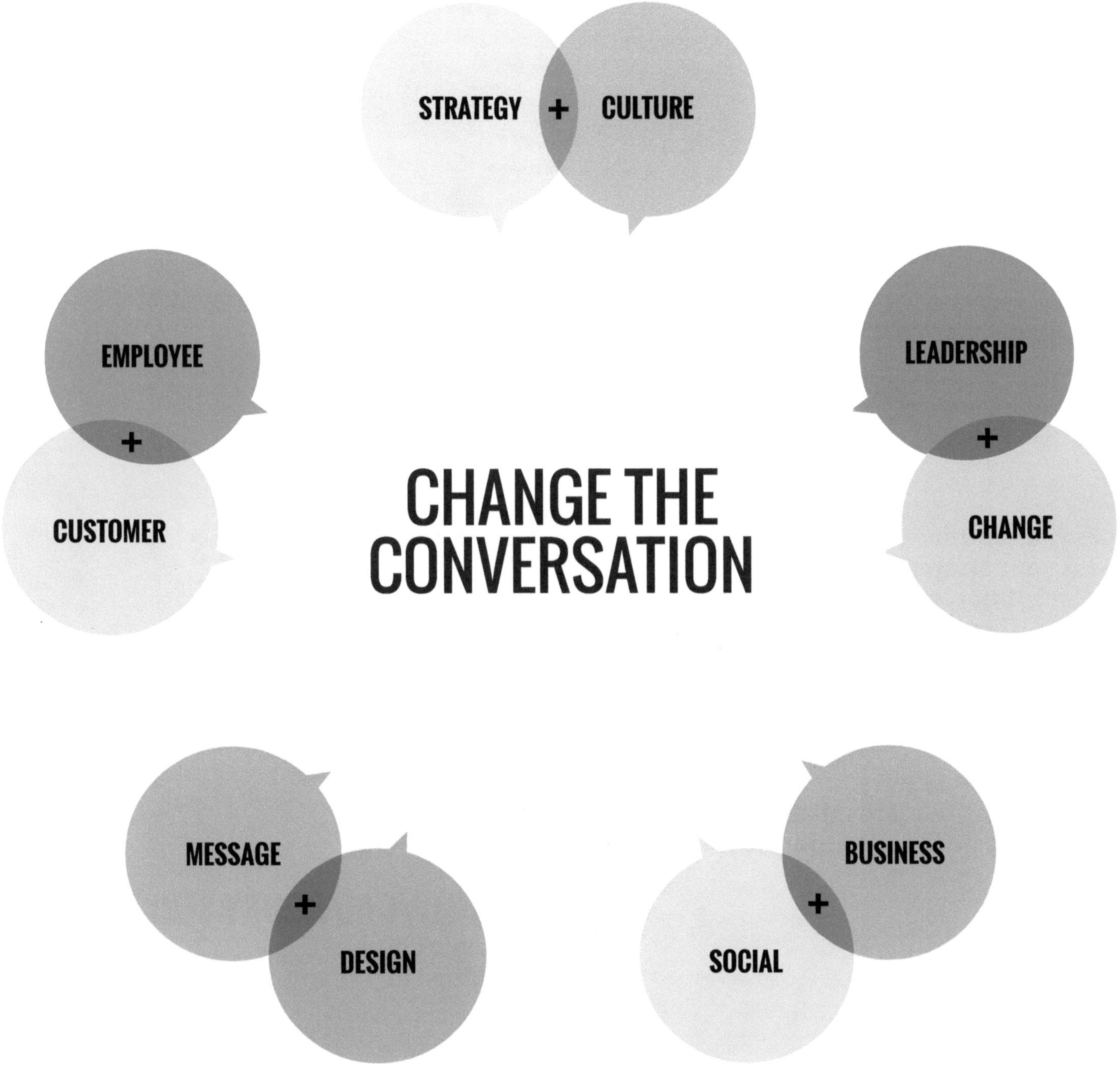

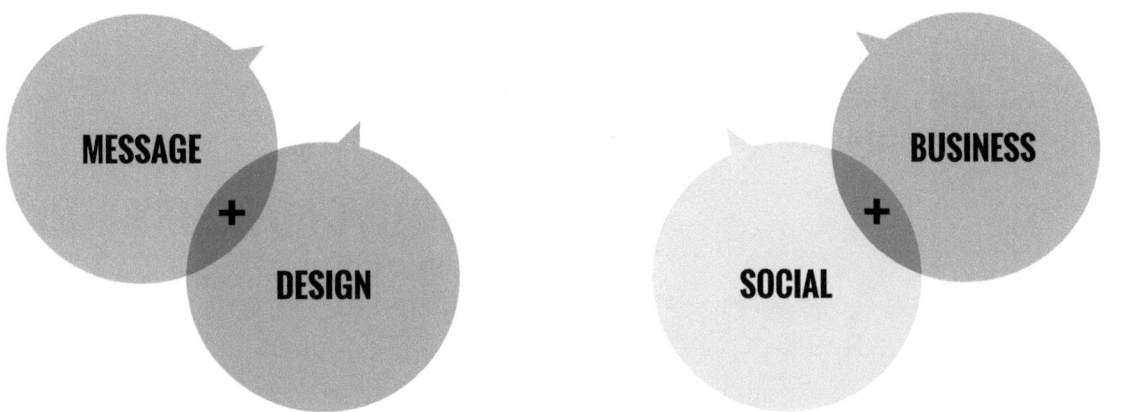

STRATEGY + CULTURE

EMPLOYEE + CUSTOMER

LEADERSHIP + CHANGE

CHANGE THE CONVERSATION

MESSAGE + DESIGN

BUSINESS + SOCIAL

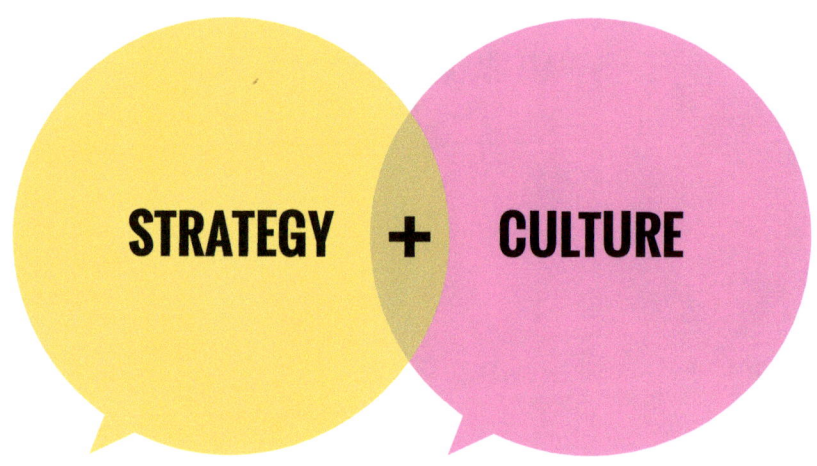

Does your culture support your strategy, and is your strategy working in your culture? **If not, you need to change the conversation.** Strategy directs what you do. Culture is how you do what you do. Execution is what you do. People factor into all three.

We identify and help you change the conversations that are hurting your culture and holding up the execution of your strategy.

STRATEGY WORKSHOPS
Culture | Strategy | Innovation

METHODS & TOOLS
Culture Audit, Organization DNA, Chocolate Conversation, Strategy Canvas, BPR

EXECUTIVE ADVISORY SERVICES
Strategic Counsel, Thinking Partnerships

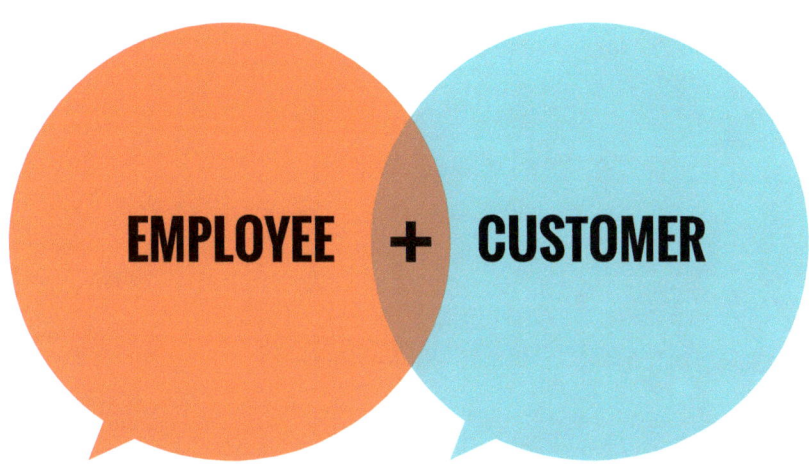

Are your employees attracting customers to your brand? Do your leaders connect the employee experience to the customer experience? **If not, you need to change the conversation.** The one leaders have with employees, employees have with customers and customers have with each other.

We help you shape and design the conversations that give employees the skill and will to positively impact the customer experience.

LEARNING LABS
Service Performance, Sales Performance, Effective Support, Customer Connection

SERVICE DESIGN
CX Metrics & Dashboards, In Store Experience, Cross-Channel Studies, Customer Journey Mapping

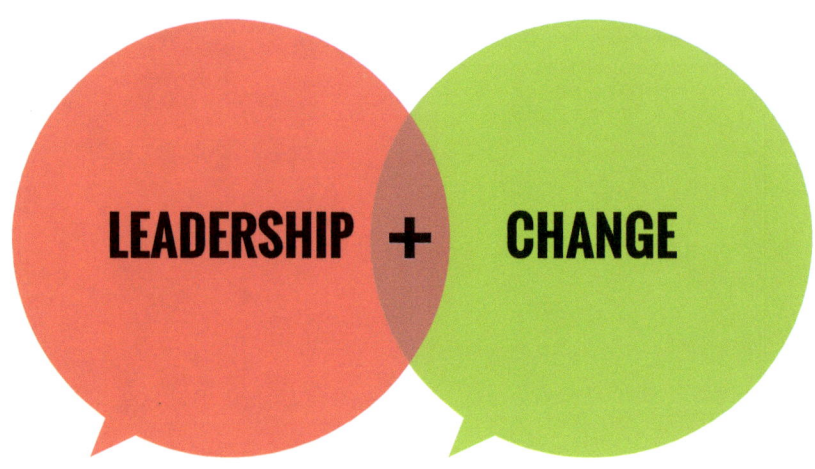

Are you leading change or is change leading you? **You need to change the conversation.** Too often leaders try to change everything, and confuse people with disconnected conversations. Conversations frame the way people see the world and leadership happens in the conversation. They set standards people live by.

We help **seasoned** leaders prepare for and have clear conversations and equip **new leaders** to make smart decisions and take action.

STRATEGY
Culture | Transformation | Performance

LEARNING LABS
Customized Leadership Universities, Leading People/ Managing Performance, Leading a Connected World, Future of Marketing

ADVISORY SERVICES
1-on-1 Leadership Development, Executive Coaching, Mentoring

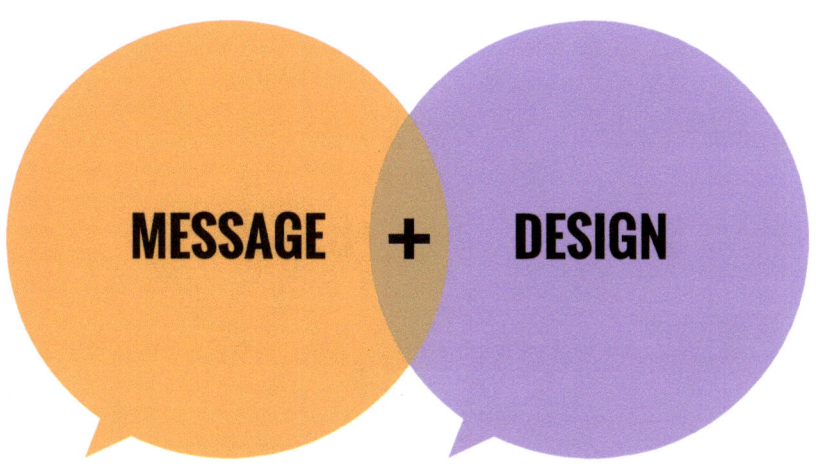

MESSAGE + DESIGN

What if everyone doesn't buy-in? **You need to change the conversation.** It doesn't matter how genius your idea, how creative your product, how precise your plan. You have to move hearts and minds. People have to see themselves in the picture, and be in the conversation with you.

We help you develop message discipline, using visuals to tell your story and build platforms that translates what you say into what people do.

STRATEGY WORKSHOPS
Vision | Brand | Message

LEARNING LABS
Presenting Better, Presenting Data, Presenting Story, Pitching to Win

VISUAL COMMUNICATION STUDIO
Presentation, Information Graphics, Pitch Decks, Data Visualization

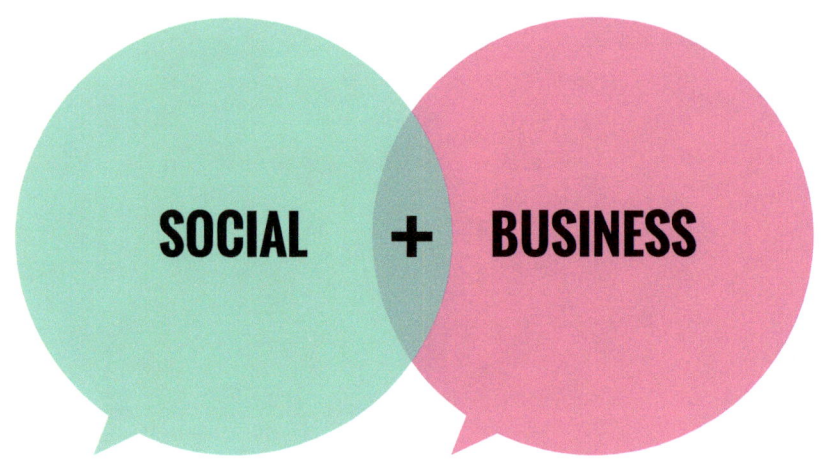

SOCIAL + **BUSINESS**

Leadership, culture and experiences have now converged to create Social Brands. Leaders of Social Brands co-create value with employees and customers by leading conversations. As a leader, are you participating in these conversations? **If not, you need to join the conversation.**

We can help you implement social business strategies that influence conversations, emphasize your culture as a differentiator and amplify what makes you better than your competition.

STRATEGY WORKSHOPS
Social Branding | Social HR

LEARNING LABS
Team Branding, Content Planning, Social Selling

ADVISORY SERVICES
Social Strategy, 1:1 Social Coaching, Executive Branding

Our clients are people and organizations who lead change and don't let change lead them. They are changing the conversation with their employees, customers, and shareholders.

WE SOLVE GRAY PROBLEMS.

The challenges you face aren't simple. They
won't be solved with black and white thinking.
We help you in the gray areas between the
seams. This is where conversations break down
and leaders usually don't want to go.

WHERE ARE YOUR SEAMS?

What

CHOCOLATE CONVERSATIONS

could you change?

Start a conversation with us at
fassforward.com